Coloring book for adults and kids bull image for design

This coloring book is
belongs to

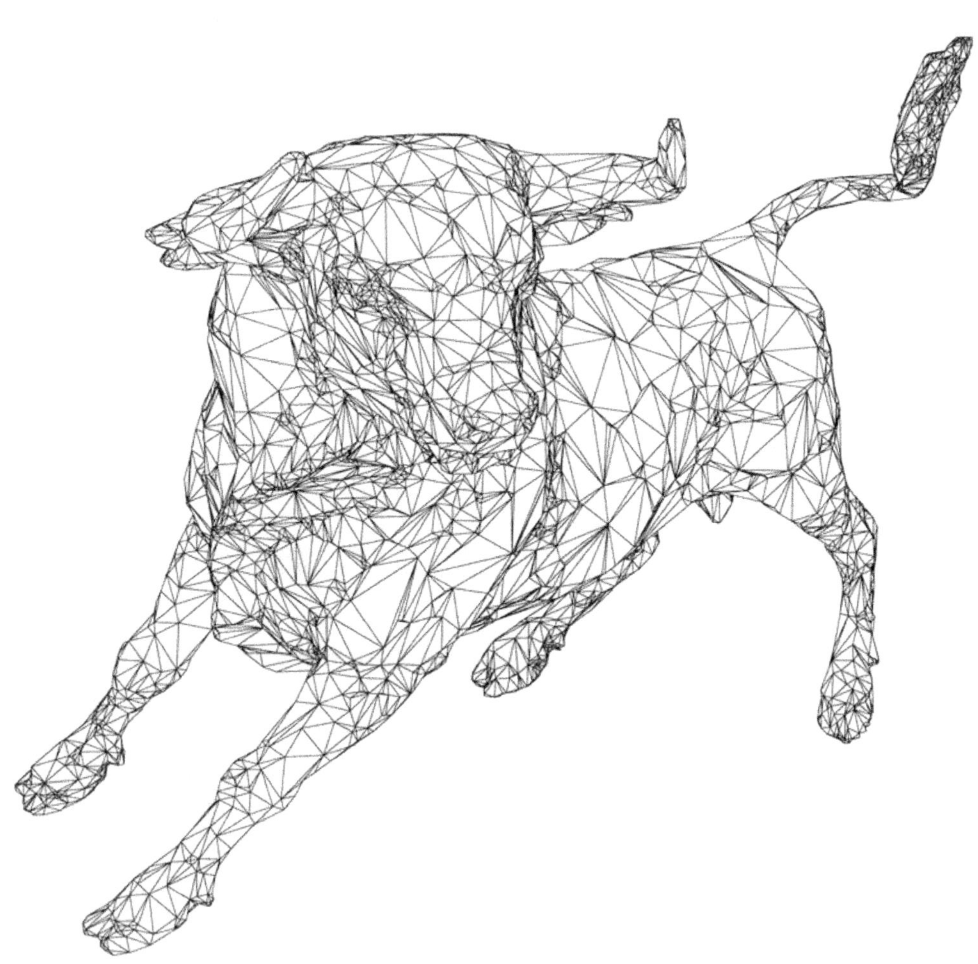

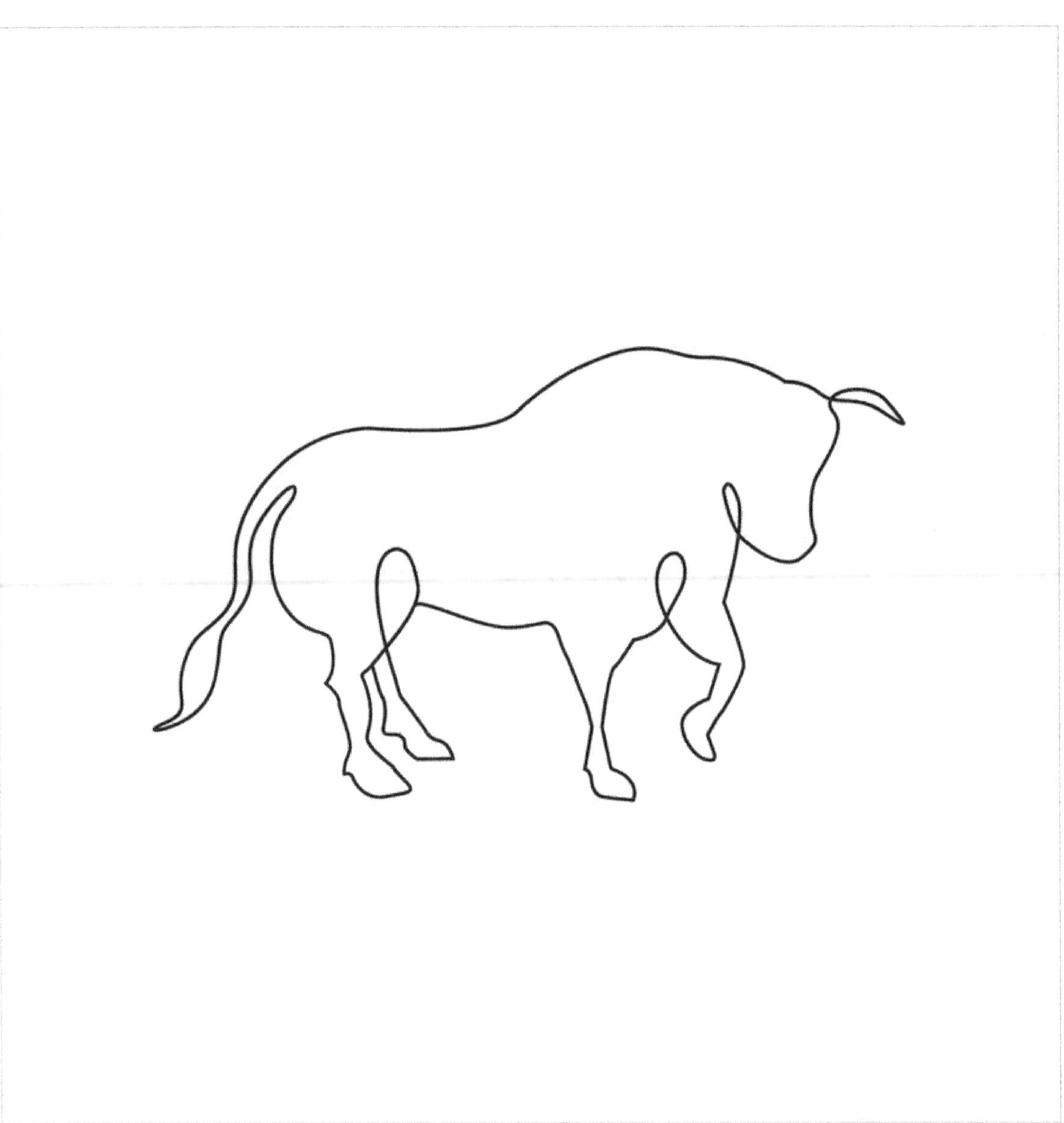

vector

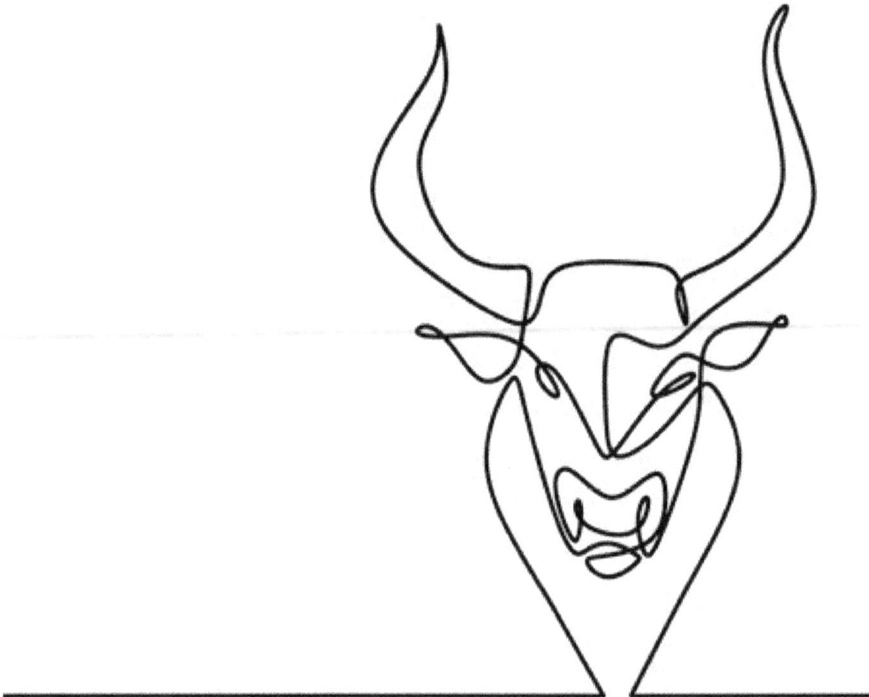

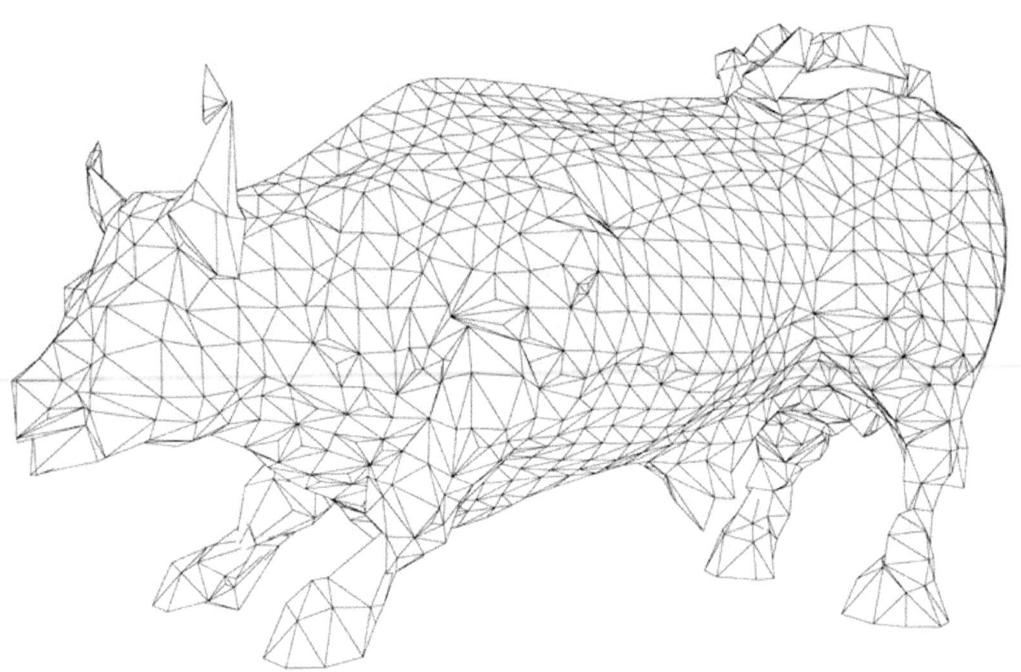

BULL

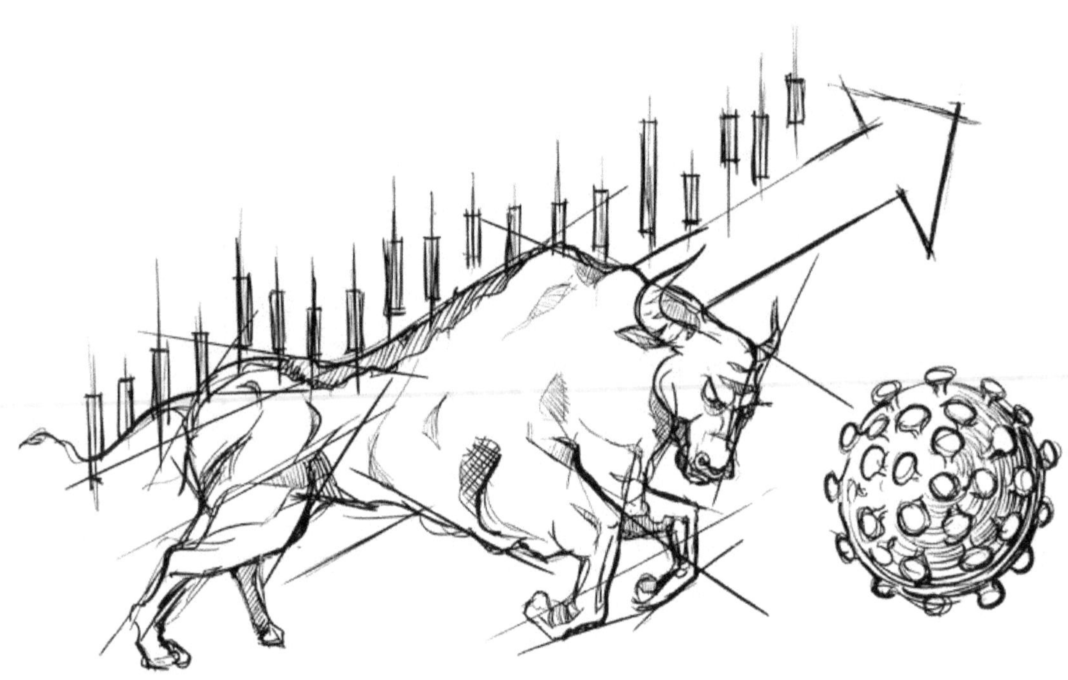

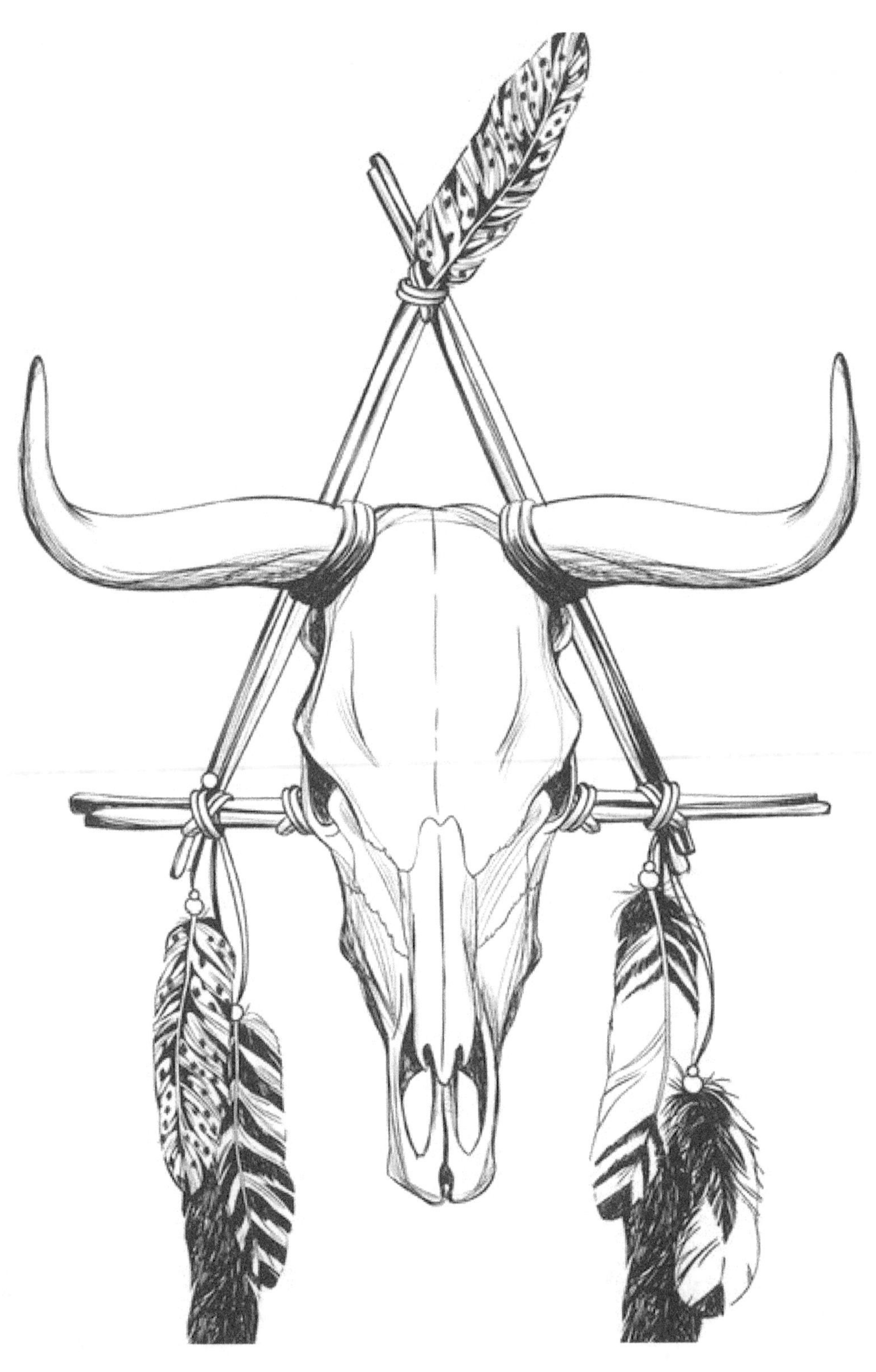

www.ingramcontent.com/pod-product-compliance
Lightning Source LLC
Chambersburg PA
CBHW081629250726
48657CB00009B/2800